It's My State!

PENNSYLVANIA

The Keystone State

Joyce Hart, Richard Hantula, and Kerry Jones Waring

Cavendish Square

New York

Published in 2015 by Cavendish Square Publishing, LLC
243 5th Avenue, Suite 136, New York, NY 10016

Website: cavendishsq.com

This publication represents the opinions and views of the author based on his or her personal experience, knowledge, and research. The information in this book serves as a general guide only. The author and publisher have used their best efforts in preparing this book and disclaim liability rising directly or indirectly from the use and application of this book.

CPSIA Compliance Information: Batch #WW15CSQ

All websites were available and accurate when this book was sent to press.

Library of Congress Cataloging-in-Publication Data

Waring, Kerry Jones.
Pennsylvania / Kerry Jones Waring, Joyce Hart, Richard Hantula. — Third Edition.
pages cm. — (It's my state!)
Includes index.
ISBN 978-1-50260-015-8 (hardcover) ISBN 978-1-50260-016-5 (ebook)
1. Pennsylvania—Juvenile literature. I. Hart, Joyce, 1954- II. Hantula, Richard. III. Title.

F149.3.W37 2014
974.8—dc23

2014021297

Editor: Fletcher Doyle
Senior Copy Editor: Wendy A. Reynolds
Art Director: Jeffrey Talbot
Designer: Doug Brooks
Senior Production Manager: Jennifer Ryder-Talbot
Production Editor: David McNamara
Photo Research by J8 Media

The photographs in this book are used by permission and through the courtesy of: Cover photo by Jerry Driendl/Getty Images; J. Paul Moore/Photolibrary/Getty Images, 4; © Wechsle, Doug / Animals Animals – Earth Scenes, 4; Getty Images: Art Wolfe, 4; Dwergenpaartje/File:Phacops rana crassituberulata dorsal.jpg/Wikimedia Commons, 5; Dave King, 5; Shutterstock: Caitlin Mirra, 5; © Matt Kazmierski, 6; Alamy: Daniel Dempster Photography, 8; H. Mark Weidman, 9; Images-USA, 12; Chuck Pefley, 13; Daderot/File:Fallingwater-DSC05639.JPG/Wikimedia Commons, 14; © iStockphoto.com/bgwalker, 14; © iStockphoto.com/bgwalker, 14;Education Images/Universal Images Group/Getty Images, 15; Ingram Publishing/Newscom, 15; Ron and Patty Thomas/Photographers Choice/Getty Images, 15; Raymond Gehman/National Geographics, 16; Delmas Lehman, 17; Stephen J. Krasemann, 18; Brandon Brown/File:Longear sunfish.jpg/Wikimedia Commons, 19; Quagell/File:Alnus incana rugosa leaves.jpg/Wikimedia Commons, 20; Adam Jones, 20; Taylor S. Kennedy/National Geographic, 20; EEI_TONY/iStock/Thinkstock, 21; Fritzflohrreynolds/File:Aquilegia canadensis - Wild Columbine 2.jpg/Wikimedia Commons, 21; Geoffrey Kuchera, 21; Three Lions/Hulton Archive, 24; Stock Montage/Hulton Archive, 25; North Wind Picture Archives, 26; Kean Collection/Hulton Archive, 28; File Fort Necessity National Battlefield FTNE2983.jpg/Wikimedia Commons, 29; val lawless/Shutterstock.com, 30; North Wind Picture Archives, 31;Smallbones/File:Delaware Canal w dog.JPG/Wikimedia Commons, 33; Doug Lemke/Shutterstock.com, 34; Bobak Ha'Eri/Philly042107-014-RockyStatue.jpg/Wikimedia Commons, 34; NFL/Getty Images, 34; nashvilledino2/iStock/Thinkstock, 35; © iStockphoto.com/billnoll, 35; Buyenlarge/Hulton Archive, 36; Ruhrfisch/File:Freedom Road Cemetery Historical Marker.JPG/Wikimedia Commons, 37; Library of Congress/Hulton Archive, 39; ArnoldReinhold/File:Univac I at CHM.agr.jpg/Wikimedia Commons, 41;H. Mark Weidman Photography, 44; Hulton Archive, 47; Kevin Mazur/WireImage/Getty Images, 48; Superstock, 48; Harry How, 48 (top); Silver Screen Collection/Moviepix/Getty Images, 49; Kevin Mazur/WireImage/Getty Images, 49; Matthew Stockman, 49 (middle); William Thomas Cain, 50; H. Mark Weidman Photography, 51;Jerry Zitterman, 52; Philip Scalia, 53; Jeff Swensen, 54; Rich Pilling/Major League Baseball, 54; William Thomas Cain/Stringer/Getty Images, 55; Wang Lei/Xinhua/Photoshot/Newscom, 55; Margie Politzer/Lonely Planet Images/Getty Images, 55; Dobresum, 56; BenC, 58; Frank Tozier, 59; Images-USA, 61; Joseph-Siggrein Duplessis/File:BenFranklinDuplessis.jpg/Wikimedia Commons, 62; Michael Ventura, 64; William Thomas Cain/Stringer/Getty Images, 66; Ken Lucas/Visuals Unlimited, 66; Semen Lixodeev, 66; Robert Nickelsberg/Getty Images, 67; Stefano Oppo/Getty Images, 67; Wade H. Massie/Shutterstock.com, 67; H. Mark Weidman, 68; Marie C Fields/Shutterstock.com, 70; Adam Crowley, 71 (Independence Hall); H. Mark Weidman, 72; Dwight Nadig/Getty Images, 75; Rdsmith4/File: Valley Forge cabin.jpg/Wikimedia Commons, 75; Mrmcdonnell/File: I80 Highest Point.jpg/Wikimedia Commons, 75.

Printed in the United States of America

PENNSYLVANIA

CONTENTS

A QUICK LOOK AT

State Tree: Eastern Hemlock

The eastern hemlock is an evergreen tree that can grow to be more than 100 feet (30 meters) tall. It thrives in almost every area of Pennsylvania. The early settlers used the wood to build their wagons, cabins, and furniture.

State Bird: Ruffed Grouse

The ruffed grouse is a plump, reddish brown bird that grows up to 19 inches (48 centimeters) long with a wingspan of up to 25 inches (64 cm). It stays low to the ground, making it easy prey for hunters.

State Flower: Mountain Laurel

In 1933, the wife of Governor Gifford Pinchot selected the mountain laurel as the official state flower—a woodland evergreen shrub with white and pink blossoms that grows in Pennsylvania forests.

PENNSYLVANIA
POPULATION: 12,702,379

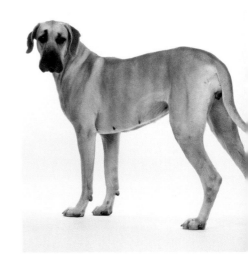

State Dog: Great Dane

Great Danes are good hunting and guard dogs. Brought over from England, they were very popular with early settlers. In 1965, the state legislature honored the Great Dane's strength and loyalty by making it Pennsylvania's official dog.

State Fossil: *Phacops rana*

More than 300 million years ago, most of Pennsylvania was under water. As a result, many of the state's fossils are sea creatures, such as the *Phacops rana*. This creature was a kind of trilobite. Trilobites were relatives of horseshoe crabs, insects, and spiders.

State Flagship: U.S. Brig *Niagara*

This large warship took part in the Battle of Lake Erie during the War of 1812. The original U.S. Brig *Niagara* eventually sank, but was raised and reconstructed in 1913. Today, it is a classroom for a sailing school.

The Fort Pitt Bridge crosses the Monongahela, one of three rivers that converge in Pittsburgh.

★ ★ ★ ★ ★

The Keystone State

L ocated in the eastern part of the United States, Pennsylvania is called the Keystone State. A keystone is a central stone in an arch. It holds the arch together. Pennsylvania got the name for two reasons. First, it was centrally located among the thirteen British colonies that combined to form the United States in the eighteenth century. Second, it played an important role in holding together the newly formed nation.

Pennsylvania is a state of differences. It is home to small towns and also large, sprawling cities, and the climate can vary greatly from region to region. These differences mean that Pennsylvanians in the eastern part of the state may live very different lives from those in the west.

Pennsylvania is a medium-size state in area. Its land area of 44,817 square miles (116,075 square kilometers) gives it a rank of thirty-second among the fifty U.S. states. However, Pennsylvania ranks sixth among the states in population. The city of Philadelphia has more than 1.5 million people, making it the sixth most populous city in the country. Pittsburgh, the state's second-largest city, has a population of about 300,000 people. The third-largest city, with more than 100,000 people, is Allentown. Pennsylvania is divided into sixty-seven counties. Harrisburg, the state capital, is located in Dauphin County, in the east-central part of the state.

Beautiful Presque Isle State Park borders Lake Erie.

The Landscape

Pennsylvania has a varied landscape, created by powerful geological forces.
Tectonic plates, the huge floating layers of rock that make up the Earth's surface, are continuously moving and crashing into each other. Millions of years ago, this activity formed mountain chains across parts of North America. Volcanoes, earthquakes, and glaciers further changed the landscape.

During the last Ice Age, a period that ended some ten thousand years ago, huge masses of moving ice, called glaciers, covered much of North America. This included the northern portion of present-day Pennsylvania. As the glaciers moved, rivers, valleys, and lakes were carved into the landscape. Through the years, wind, water, and other natural forces continued to shape the land. As a result, Pennsylvania's landscape today includes flat plains, gently rolling hills, valleys, and mountain chains.

The northwestern corner of the state is part of the Great Lakes Plain, which hugs the shores of Lake Erie. Lake Erie is one of the five Great Lakes and, in area, is the eleventh-largest lake in the world. The Great Lakes Plain is a relatively flat strip of land. The city of Erie is located here. With about 100,000 people, it is Pennsylvania's major port on the lake.

The edge of the plain gives way to the Appalachian **Plateau**, sometimes called the Allegheny Plateau in this region. A plateau is a mass of land that rises above the land surrounding it. Its sides often look like steep walls. Some plateaus are flat along the top, but the Appalachian Plateau has a rather rugged top. The Appalachian Plateau covers most of the western and northern portions of the state and is the location of many state parks and forests, as well as a national forest. Relatively few people live in this region, but the area is famous for its deposits of coal and oil.

The Appalachian Plateau gradually increases in height and becomes part of the Appalachian Mountains—a large chain of mountains that runs from southeastern Canada down to central Alabama. Many geologists believe this mountain range is one of the oldest in the world. More than 200 million years ago, the Appalachian Mountains were more than 15,000 feet (4,500 meters) high.

Hikers in the Allegheny State Forest in the northwest can see many kinds of plant and animal life.

PENNSYLVANIA
POPULATION BY COUNTY

County	Population	County	Population	County	Population
Adams County	101, 407	Elk County	31,946	Montour County	18,267
Allegheny County	1,223,348	Erie County	280,566	Northampton County	297,735
Armstrong County	68,941	Fayette County	136,606	Northumberland County	94,528
Beaver County	170,539	Forest County	7,716	Perry County	45,969
Bedford County	49,762	Franklin County	149,618	Philadelphia County	1,526,006
Berks County	411,442	Fulton County	14,845	Pike County	57,369
Blair County	127,089	Greene County	38,686	Potter County	17,457
Bradford County	62,622	Huntingdon County	45,913	Schuylkill County	148,289
Bucks County	625,249	Indiana County	88,880	Snyder County	39,702
Butler County	183,862	Jefferson County	45,200	Somerset County	77,742
Cambria County	143,679	Juniata County	24,636	Sullivan County	6,428
Cameron County	5,085	Lackawanna County	214,437	Susquehanna County	43,356
Carbon County	65,249	Lancaster County	519,445	Tioga County	41,981
Centre County	153,990	Lawrence County	91,108	Union County	44,947
Chester County	498,886	Lebanon County	133,568	Venango County	54,984
Clarion County	39,988	Lehigh County	349,497	Warren County	41,815
Clearfield County	81,642	Luzerne County	320,918	Washington County	207,820
Clinton County	39,238	Lycoming County	116,111	Wayne County	52,822
Columbia County	67,295	McKean County	43,450	Westmoreland County	365,169
Crawford County	88,765	Mercer County	116,638	Wyoming County	28,276
Cumberland County	235,406	Mifflin County	46,682	York County	434,972
Dauphin County	268,100	Monroe County	169,842		
Delaware County	558,979	Montgomery County	799,874		

Source: U.S. Bureau of the Census, 2010

The Allegheny Mountain Tunnel on the Pennsylvania Turnpike is more than a mile (1.6 km) long.

The portion of the Appalachians that begins in central Pennsylvania and runs to the southwest is called the Allegheny Mountains. The Alleghenies include the highest point in Pennsylvania, Mount Davis, which stands 3,213 feet (979 m) high.

Through the years, however, earthquakes and volcanic activity changed the features of the mountains. Glaciers that moved through the area during the Ice Age further eroded—or wore away—the mountain peaks. Rain and wind continued to eat away at the mountains, leveling them to their current heights.

Pittsburgh lies in the northern foothills of the Alleghenies, where the Monongahela and Allegheny rivers come together to form the Ohio River. According to one recent count, it has the most bridges of any city in the world, slightly ahead of Venice and Hamburg, Germany.

The Alleghenies give way to a series of smaller mountain ranges, including the Jacks, the

Pennsylvania Borders

North:	New York
	Lake Erie
South:	Delaware
	Maryland
	West Virginia
East:	New York
	New Jersey
West:	Ohio
	West Virginia

Tuscarora, and the Blue mountains. These ranges are located in an area known as the Great Valley region. Harrisburg is located on the Susquehanna River in the Great Valley region. The city of Allentown, on the Lehigh River, is also in the Great Valley.

Moving eastward from the Alleghenies and the Great Valley region, the land flattens out and becomes level at the Piedmont Plateau. The Piedmont extends from Pennsylvania into New Jersey and Maryland, and it continues south toward Alabama. In Pennsylvania, the Piedmont Plateau is not as rugged as the Appalachian Plateau. Instead, it is a landscape of rolling hills and fertile soil. Many of Pennsylvania's farms are located here.

The southeastern corner of the state is part of the Atlantic Coastal Plain, which stretches down the eastern edge of the United States from New York to Florida. Like the Great Lakes Plain, the Atlantic Coastal Plain is mostly very flat and very fertile. It is home to Philadelphia. The city lies on the Delaware River, which separates Pennsylvania from New Jersey.

Waterways

From recreation to industry, waterways are an important part of life in Pennsylvania. Pennsylvania is dotted with lakes. Some are natural lakes formed over many years of

Philadelphia, which is on the Delaware River, is one of the largest cities in the United States.

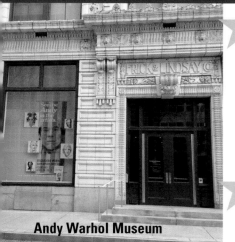

Andy Warhol Museum

1. The Andy Warhol Museum

Andy Warhol, an American artist who lived from 1928 to 1987, was a leading figure in the Pop Art movement. Located in Pittsburgh, the country's largest museum devoted to a single artist includes 900 paintings, approximately 100 sculptures, and 4,000 photographs.

2. Fallingwater

Built over a waterfall in Mill Run, Fallingwater was designed by Frank Lloyd Wright, one of America's most famous architects. Fallingwater was built between 1936 and 1939, and today it is a National Historic Landmark.

Fallingwater

3. Gettysburg National Military Park

Gettysburg was the site of one of the Civil War's most important battles, fought July 1 through July 3, 1863. Visit the battlefield and surrounding landmarks, including the Soldiers' National Cemetery, where President Abraham Lincoln gave the Gettysburg Address.

4. Hersheypark

Established in 1907 by the Hershey Chocolate Company's founder, Milton Hershey, as a place for his employees to relax with their families, this theme park in Derry Township features more than 65 rides and attractions, and hosts nearly three million people every year.

5. Lancaster County

Also called Pennsylvania Dutch Country, Lancaster County is home to many **Amish** people, a group known for simple living, plain dress, and for not using many forms of modern technology, as well as for their homemade goods.

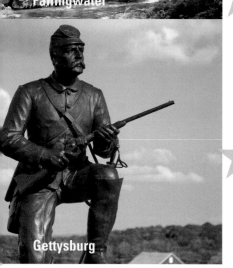

Gettysburg

6. Liberty Bell

This symbol of American independence, located in Philadelphia, was created in 1752. The Liberty Bell is famous for a crack in its surface that appeared the first time it was rung, and which remains to this day.

7. National Watch and Clock Museum

Home to the largest collection of timepieces in North America, Columbia's National Watch and Clock Museum features clocks, watches, tools and other items from around the world. Each exhibit takes you on a tour through the history of timekeeping.

8. Pocono Mountains

The Poconos mountain range covers more than 2,400 square miles (6,215 sq. km) in northeastern Pennsylvania. Mountains, waterfalls, woodlands, and rivers make the area a popular location for skiing, hiking, bicycling, whitewater rafting, and other outdoor activities.

9. Presque Isle State Park

Presque Isle State Park is a 3,200-acre (1,295 hectares) sandy peninsula on Lake Erie. Containing 21 miles (33.79 km) of trails, thirteen beaches, a marina and more, it is home to a large number of the state's endangered, threatened, and rare species of animals.

10. Peter J. McGovern Little League Museum

Located in South Williamsport and opened in 1982, the museum houses artifacts and information about the history of youth baseball and its role in American and world history. It also hosts the Little League World Series.

Liberty Bell

The Poconos

Little League Museum

A kayaker battles the Susquehanna River as it passes under the Rockville Bridge. It was the longest stone archway bridge in the world when it was built in the early 1900s.

geologic change. Others are artificial lakes, created to keep Pennsylvania's rivers from flooding. Pennsylvania's largest natural lake is Conneaut Lake in the northwestern part of the state.

Many rivers flow through the mountains, creating some of the most beautiful waterfalls on the East Coast. The rivers of Pennsylvania provided a major means of transportation for many years. Their usefulness was greatly increased by a series of human-made canals that were constructed as early as 1797. These canals bypassed rapids and falls, and they connected rivers. They allowed people and cargo to travel over rugged land features such as parts of the Alleghenies. Large floods have destroyed some canals, but historical markers point out where many of the canals were dug.

Pennsylvanians love to have fun on the water, too. Presque Isle State Park, located on Lake Erie, and the Pocono Mountain region are both great locations for outdoor fun like swimming and whitewater rafting.

The Climate

Because Pennsylvania has so many different kinds of geographic features, the weather in one region can be very different from other parts of the state in the same season. Overall, Pennsylvania enjoys four distinct weather seasons.

Summers are long, hot and humid, particularly in the southeast around Philadelphia. The mountainous areas are likely to be cooler and less humid. Autumns are pleasant statewide, while winters, especially in the mountains, are cold and snowy. Snowfalls can top 100 inches (254 cm) a year. Lake Erie keeps the northwest corner cooler and regulates the change of seasons. July tends to be the state's warmest month as temperatures can top 90 degrees Fahrenheit (32 degrees Celsius) in the southeast and southwestern areas and average 80°F (27°C). January is the coldest month, with temperatures falling to about 23°F (–5°C).

Wildlife

Pennsylvania's forests are home to trees such as maple, oak, birch, pine, and elm. In the fall, Pennsylvania forests and hills turn lovely shades of orange, red, and yellow as the leaves change colors. Flowers bloom alongside the trees. Pennsylvania's state flower, the mountain laurel, grows wild in the forests, as do azaleas and rhododendrons.

State Conservation Plant

The state of Pennsylvania has an official beautification and conservation plant: the hardy Penngift crownvetch. It features pink and white flowers and is often planted along roadsides and in other places not only for decoration but to help control erosion. It is also used for livestock feed.

There are more historic covered bridges in Pennsylvania than in any other state.

Pennsylvania's forests and fields are also home to rabbits, raccoons, opossums, deer, squirrels, and bats. The white-tailed deer can be found nearly everywhere and is the official state animal. On a nature hike, visitors might also spot beavers, minks, woodchucks, and chipmunks. Black bears and bobcats were once almost extinct in the state, but their numbers have increased.

The state is also home to many different types of birds. There are plenty of wild turkeys and ruffed grouse. Ducks, geese, and herons can be found feeding at the state's waterways. Robins, sparrows, larks, chickadees, owls, hawks, and falcons may be seen in the skies or perched in the trees.

Endangered Wildlife

Many species—or types—of plants and animals that lived in the state hundreds or thousands of years ago are no longer around. This is mostly because of human settlement in the region. Forests were cut down and waterways were rerouted, destroying the natural homes and food sources of many animals. Overhunting and pollution have also affected certain animal species. They have become endangered—that is, in danger of dying out or disappearing from the state.

Some species have been saved from becoming extinct (dying out). Bald eagles used to fly across Pennsylvania skies and nest in the tall trees. However, for most of the twentieth

Wild turkeys are common around Pennsylvania.

century, there were no bald eagles left in the state. Laws were passed restricting people from harming these eagles. Conservation efforts to breed and release these striking birds began. As a result, the population slowly began to increase. Today, you might see bald eagles living in watery areas in most of the state's counties. Elk are another example. These animals have twice become almost extinct in the Allegheny Mountains. But today, Pennsylvania has several hundred elk.

A number of species of plants and animals are still endangered in Pennsylvania. Among them are birds such as the short-eared owl, mammals such as the Delmarva fox squirrel, and some types of sturgeons, shiners, sunfish, and other fish.

A Friendly Rivalry

The distinct weather, landscapes, and cultures of regions of Pennsylvania may play a role in the rivalry that exists between its largest cities, Pittsburgh and Philadelphia. This rivalry can be seen when the cities' professional sports teams play—especially in hockey [the Pittsburgh Penguins and the Philadelphia Flyers] and baseball [the Philadelphia Phillies and Pittsburgh Pirates].

The longear sunfish is among the endangered species in the state.

Firefly

Great Blue Heron

Speckled Alder

1. Blackberries

Blackberry bushes grow wild in the mountainous regions of Pennsylvania. Their hedges of tangled brambles offer great hiding places for small forest creatures. In the spring, blackberry flowers bloom, and in the late summer, sweet berries grow on the branches.

2. Brook Trout

Found in Pennsylvania's cool lakes and streams, brook trout are very colorful fish, with light-green backs highlighted with yellow and black spots. They are the only trout native to Pennsylvania streams. The brook trout is Pennsylvania's official state fish.

3. Firefly

On summer nights, most fields in Pennsylvania are filled with the blinking lights of fireflies. Fireflies use their flashing light to scare away predators, and to attract a mate. The *Photuris pennsylvanica* De Geer firefly is the state's official insect.

4. Great Blue Heron

The largest member of the heron family in North America, great blue herons can be more than 3 feet (1 m) tall. An excellent fisher, it wades in shallow water to catch fish with its long, sharp beak.

5. Speckled Alder

As a deciduous plant, speckled adler lose and regain their leaves every year and can grow to be 20 feet (6.1 m) tall. Birds eat the seeds and buds of the plant, while beavers often use its wood to build dams.

PENNSYLVANIA

6. Striped Skunk

Found in forests and near farmland, striped skunks eat insects, fruits, plants, and sometimes mice. These little creatures release a very strong scent that most animals—including humans—cannot stand when frightened or threatened.

Striped Skunk

7. Sugar Maple

Sugar maples can grow to be 80 feet (24.3 m) tall. Maple syrup is made from its sap, and its wood is used in furniture. Birds and rodents eat the seeds, and deer and other mammals eat the twigs, buds and bark.

8. Switch Grass

Found in Presque Isle State Park, switch grass plays an important role in preserving the natural beauty of Pennsylvania's beaches. The roots of this grass provide erosion control, keeping sand in place and protecting it against wind and water.

White-Tailed Deer

9. White-Tailed Deer

The white underside of Pennsylvania's official state animal's tail is easily visible when it runs and serves as a warning to others when danger is sensed. White-tailed deer can run up to 40 miles per hour (64 km/h), and are fast swimmers.

10. Wild Columbine

Pennsylvania is home to wild columbine, a boldly colored flower with yellow petals and red markings. Butterflies and hummingbirds love it for its sweet nectar. Wild columbine is a perennial, meaning the same plant will return to grow each spring.

Wild Columbine

William Penn meets Lenape Chief Tammany in a painting by Benjamin West.

From the Beginning

2

Pennsylvania has a rich and interesting history, created by the different people who have lived in the region: Native Americans; English, Dutch, Swedish, and German settlers; and many others. Their experiences and influences have shaped the state into what it is today.

The Europeans

The region that would become Pennsylvania played an important role in the history of European settlers in America. Many historians believe that English captain John Smith was the first European to visit the region. Smith is believed to have sailed up the Susquehanna River and met with the Susquehannock people in 1608.

A year later, the Dutch government hired Henry Hudson to sail to North America in search of a water route to Asia. Hudson sailed into Delaware Bay and claimed the surrounding land on behalf of the Dutch. Other Dutch explorers soon came and set up trading posts there, but they did not construct permanent settlements.

In 1638, an expedition from Sweden arrived and claimed ownership of the region. They called the area Nya Sverige, which meant "New Sweden." Tinicum Island, in the Delaware River, was later named the capital of the Swedish territory. (Today the site is part of Pennsylvania. It is located southwest of present-day Philadelphia.) In 1654, the Swedes captured a Dutch fort in what is now Delaware, but Swedish control was short-lived. The following year, the Dutch reclaimed the entire region for their government.

Then, in 1664, the English decided that they wanted the land and claimed the same area for the Duke of York. The English gained and maintained control of the region. Nearly twenty years later, the English king, Charles II, gave William Penn a portion of that land. This portion later became Pennsylvania.

The Charter of Pennsylvania

William Penn was a **Quaker**—a member of a religious group called the Society of Friends. The Quakers were not treated well in England, and Penn wanted to establish a new colony where Quakers—and others—could live peacefully and worship as they pleased. He asked King Charles II to grant him land west of the Delaware River for this purpose. The king agreed, both because he owed money to Penn's father and because he wanted to honor the father's loyal service as an admiral. Charles II signed the land grant in 1681.

This grant, called the Charter of Pennsylvania, gave Penn the right to establish a colony in North America. The king named the colony Pennsylvania ("Penn's woods"), in honor of William Penn's father.

King Charles II presents a charter to William Penn, allowing him to found the colony of Pennsylvania.

Penn, as proprietor, or governor, arrived in 1682. Together with other settlers, he organized the local government using a constitution that he called the Frame of Government. This document stated that people had a right to own land and to govern themselves. "Any government is free to the people under it . . . where the laws rule, and the people are a party to those laws," it said.

(Self-government was a new concept for most Europeans, as many European countries at that time were ruled by kings and queens.)

Penn also helped plan the city of Philadelphia. He chose its name, which means "brotherly love" in Greek. The city was central to Pennsylvania society, and it grew to become the largest city in the American colonies.

Penn became very sick in 1712 and was no longer able to carry out his duties as proprietor, or governor, of Pennsylvania. His wife, Hannah, took over and ran the colony until her death in 1726.

Colonial Wars

The population of Pennsylvania continued to grow, but most of the new settlers lived in what is now eastern Pennsylvania. Westward expansion was limited by the thick forests, the mountains, and a lack of roads wide enough to allow the passage of horse-drawn wagons. However, some settlers did venture west in search of more land.

Both France and Britain wanted control of the land west of the established colonies, in spite of

(From left) Benjamin Franklin, Thomas Jefferson, John Adams, Robert Livingston, and Roger Sherman discuss the recently completed Declaration of Independence.

The Native People

Native Americans lived in what is now Pennsylvania for thousands of years before the first Europeans arrived. The original tribes include the Erie, Iroquois—especially the Seneca and the Oneida—the Lenape, the Munsee, the Shawnee and the Susquehannock. They all spoke Algonquian languages. The Susquehannock, who lived along the Susquehanna River, were known as fierce warriors and they traded animal hides and other goods for European supplies such as cloth and tools. The Lenape and Munsee, who considered themselves related, lived in the Eastern part of the state near the Delaware River. The Erie and the Iroquois live along the New York border, and the Shawnee in the central and western parts of presentday Pennsylvania.

These tribes moved with the seasons. In the summer, they might live near the rivers, where they could catch fish. In the fall, they might move toward the mountains, where they could eat wild berries, nuts, and other plants. The men did the hunting, and the women did the farming, growing corn, beans and squash, and the home chores. They wore animal-skin clothing, sometimes decorated with beads, and lived in wigwams

The Iroquois built longhouses that could hold many people.

made of poles covered with bark. Sometimes they protected their villages with palisades or log walls. They used dugout canoes to travel on the region's many rivers.

Despite the efforts of a few groups of European settlers, in particular the Quakers, to treat the Native Americans fairly, almost all of the original inhabitants of Pennsylvania were driven west in the 1700s, eventually being settled in Oklahoma. The Shawnee moved to Ohio after the American Revolution before being forced out. The Susquehannock were nearly wiped out by epidemics, although the final group of twenty was massacred in 1763 by a mob.

Today, there are no federally recognized tribes in Pennsylvania. The Lenape entered a union with the Cherokee in Oklahoma, and didn't regain their independent tribal status until 1996. There are about 16,000 surviving Lenape, with a few living in communities in New Jersey and Pennsylvania.

Spotlight on the Lenape

The Lenape tribe has called the region of Pennsylvania home for over 10,000 years.

Clans: The Lenape were divided into three clans, known as Wolf, Turtle, and Turkey. Families were important to the Lenape way of life. Lenape communities could vary in size from small groups of twenty-five to thirty people to large villages of 200 people.

Homes: Many Lenape families lived in wigwams, round houses built with wood branches and covered with bark or animal hide. Some lived in longhouses, a rectangular structure that usually had a high roof and no windows.

Entertainment: Men and boys played lacrosse, while both boys and girls played a game in which a ball was kicked. Men and women contributed in storytelling, art, and music.

Clothing: Much of the clothing worn by the Lenape was made from animal hides. Men wore breechcloths, also known as loincloths, moccasins, and animal skin robes in the winter. Women wore similar robes with knee-length skirts, and sometimes jewelry made of animal bone or shell. The women carried their babies on their backs in cradleboards.

Art: The Lenape are known for their beadwork and basketmaking. They also crafted *wampum*, beads made out of shells. The designs on beadwork or wampum often told a story.

the fact that the area was already inhabited by Native Americans. French and British newcomers started settlements there. Both countries built military forts in the region. This included land that is now part of western Pennsylvania. From 1689 to 1763, France and Britain fought over land rights in a series of four wars.

As the tensions between the French and British grew, some Native American groups took sides with one or the other country. In 1754, the French and Indian War—the last of the four wars—broke out. One of the first battles of this war was fought at Fort Necessity, near Farmington. There, the French and their Native allies defeated a force of British and colonial men commanded by George Washington. It was the only time in his military career that Washington surrendered to an enemy. The site is now Fort Necessity National Battlefield.

The French and Indian War lasted nine years. In the end, Britain won. As a result of the 1763 treaty ending the war, the British controlled land in Canada, a large amount of land between the colonies and the Mississippi River, and some land in what is now Florida.

Moving Toward Independence

By the mid-1700s, many colonists were unhappy with British control. They did not like Britain's taxes and trade rules. Many wanted the colonies to become independent and govern themselves. In 1774, representatives from most of the American colonies met in Philadelphia for the First Continental Congress. They decided that the colonies would no longer trade with Britain.

George Washington's unsuccessful attempt to save Fort Necessity came early in the French and Indian War.

By April 1775, the American Revolution had begun, and colonists were fighting the British. A month after the start of the war, the Second Continental Congress began meeting in Philadelphia. The following year, it voted for independence from Britain and issued the Declaration of Independence, which stated that the rights of the colonies had been denied so they were declaring themselves independent and no longer tied to Britain.

Though colonial forces won some battles at the beginning of the war, the colonists' Continental Army faced many problems fighting the British. The British military men were well trained and had spent years fighting in or preparing to fight in battles. Most colonial soldiers were craftsmen or farmers or had held other nonmilitary jobs. Fighting and traveling from battle to battle was new to them. At first, these colonists did not have good weapons or the skills to use them. Over time, they grew stronger and more skilled, but battles against the British were still very difficult to win.

A few major battles in the American Revolution occurred in Pennsylvania. In September 1777, General George Washington and his men fought British troops at the Battle of Brandywine. Washington's men were forced to retreat. Later that month, the British soundly defeated a colonial force led by General Anthony Wayne in the

Children can attend reenactments of the battle at Fort Necessity.

Making a Potato Letterpress Stamp

Benjamin Franklin is one of America's founding fathers and a famed resident of Philadelphia. Among his many professions, which also included author, scientist, and inventor, Franklin was a successful editor and printer who printed many Pennsylvanian newspapers. Franklin used **letterpress stamps** to print his newspapers. While those stamps were often made from wood, you can create your own letterpress stamps with just a few items from around the house.

What You Need

Unpeeled potatoes (One potato makes two stamps)

A small knife—only to be used with an adult's help

Spoon

A marker

Poster, tempera, or acrylic paint

Paper

A paper plate or bowl

What To Do

- Wash the outside of the potatoes to ensure no dirt or fibers end up in your paint.

- With an adult's help, cut each potato in half.

- On the white part of the potato, use your marker to draw the letter or shape you want to make as your stamp. Make sure to make big, block letters or shapes that are easy to carve around.

- Using the spoon, carve away the potato around the letter or shape you drew. You only need to carve about a quarter-inch deep into the potato.

- Pour paint into the plate or bowl.

- Dip the potato stamp into the paint and then press it onto the paper.

- Tip: Potato stamps can be reused if paint is rinsed off completely and carefully.

Battle of Paoli near Philadelphia, and a few days after that, the British took over the city. Washington's forces again faced British troops near Philadelphia at the Battle of Germantown in October. The British won the battle, and the colonial army had to retreat.

The following winter months were difficult for many colonial troops. Starting in mid-December, Washington and his men stayed in Valley Forge, located northwest of Philadelphia. His army was cold, tired, and hungry. The men did not have enough warm clothing, blankets, or food. During the winter at Valley Forge, many soldiers died from illness. Others deserted—or ran away from—the army.

In February 1778, conditions began to improve. More supplies were brought in. Baron Friedrich von Steuben, a military man from Prussia (an area largely in the present-day country of Germany), volunteered to help train Washington's men. By spring of that year, they had regained their strength and confidence, and they continued to fight British forces. With help from France, the colonial armies made progress against the British. The British forces left Philadelphia in June.

Colonial troops battled the British at Brandywine, but had to retreat.

As the fighting continued, the British found allies among some Native American tribes. In July 1778, some Iroquois in the region joined with the British to fight groups of settlers living in eastern Pennsylvania. The area, known as the Wyoming Valley, is near present-day Wilkes-Barre. A few hundred colonial troops and settlers were killed during the Wyoming Valley Massacre, and many settlers fled. In turn, colonial forces later destroyed several Iroquois villages in the area.

Pennsylvania did make one major and unique contribution to the war effort. The Pennsylvania Long Rifle was developed in the early 1700s. Historians credit Martin Mylin, who came to Lancaster County from Germany, with inventing this gun. The gun barrel was longer than those on the muskets used by the British forces. It was also rifled, which means there were spiral grooves inside the barrel that gave spin to the bullet. This spin makes the bullet fly straighter and makes the gun more accurate.

The gun could shoot five times farther than the British muskets. Its range was about three hundred yards (274 meters), and it was very accurate. This allowed soldiers from the colonial army to hide in wooded areas and hit enemy targets while staying out of range of the British guns. Use of this tactic helped win the first Battle of Saratoga in 1777, one of the turning points of the war.

The American Revolution officially ended in 1783, and the colonies became an independent nation, the United States of America. In Philadelphia, a national constitution was written in 1787, after much debate at the Constitutional Convention that met there from May to September. Then the colonies began to ratify, or approve, the document. Pennsylvania was the second state (after Delaware) to approve the Constitution, doing so on December 12, 1787. Philadelphia served as the capital of the new nation from 1790 to 1800, when the national government moved to Washington, D.C.

The 1800s

Pennsylvania continued to grow and prosper into the 1800s. Cities flourished, farms thrived, and industry expanded. Pennsylvania manufactured a large portion of the country's goods. Its steel mills, coal mines, and factories helped the economy. Pennsylvania was also well known for its glass production.

Pennsylvania's waterways were important for the transportation of people and goods. The state's first canal, the Conewago Canal, on the west bank of the Susquehanna River, was completed in 1797. About 1 mile (1.6 km) long, it allowed boats to bypass rocks and rapids in the Susquehanna and travel from York Haven to Columbia by water. More canal systems were established to improve travel and trade. In 1825, the Schuylkill Canal, actually a collection of separate canals and dam-created pools, became the first long canal project in Pennsylvania.

By 1828, it measured 108 miles (174 km) in length, stretching from Port Carbon via Reading to Philadelphia, and it was used mainly to carry coal. Then, in 1834, the Pennsylvania Canal, which included a railroad segment that went up one side of the mountains and down the other, began enabling people and goods to more easily cross the Alleghenies. A series of large floods eventually destroyed many of the canals, but a few stretches of the Pennsylvania Canal have been preserved or restored. Railroads were expanded in the state in the 1850s, further improving Pennsylvania's transportation system.

End of Slavery

It is hereby enacted . . . That all Persons, as well Negroes, and Mulattos, as others, who shall be born within this State, from and after the Passing of this Act, shall not be deemed and considered as Servants for Life or Slaves.

—From An Act for the Gradual Abolition of Slavery, 1780

Delaware Canal State Park in Bristol is close to the southern end of the Delaware Canal, which runs to Easton in the north.

10 KEY CITIES

Philadelphia Museum of Art

Pittsburgh's Heinz Field

Erie

1. Philadelphia: population 1,526,006

Pennsylvania's largest metropolis is known as the "City of Brotherly Love"—the translation of its name from Greek. Founded in 1682, it was the site of many important moments in American history, including the signing of the Declaration of Independence.

2. Pittsburgh: population 305,704

Pittsburgh's legacy as a major site for steel manufacturing is the origin of its nickname—the Steel City—and the name of its NFL team, the Steelers. Today, Pittsburgh's economy is based largely on healthcare, education, and technology.

3. Allentown: population 118,032

Allentown is the largest city in the Lehigh Valley region, and was formally incorporated as a city in 1867. During the Revolutionary War, the Liberty Bell was hidden successfully from British troops in the basement of Zion Reformed Church.

4. Erie: population 101,786

Located on Lake Erie, this city's population has seen a large influx of resettled refugees from Bosnia, Ghana, Iraq, Somalia and more since the mid-1990s. The city boasts a diverse economy that includes healthcare, insurance, and plastics manufacturing.

5. Reading: population 88,082

Reading is located approximately halfway between Philadelphia and Harrisburg. This location was key to the success of the now-defunct Reading Railroad, founded in 1833. The railroad transported **anthracite coal** throughout the eastern United States.

6. Scranton: population 76,089

Nicknamed the Electric City after Dickson Locomotive Works introduced electric lights in 1880, Scranton was the site of the nation's first successful electrified streetcars in 1886. Vice President Joe Biden's birthplace was also the setting for the television sitcom *The Office*.

Harrisburg

7. Bethlehem: population 74,982

The city is located in the center of the Lehigh Valley region. Its most famous company was the Bethlehem Steel Corporation, which was the nation's second-largest producer of steel before reduced demand and increased competition forced it to close in the 1990s.

8. Lancaster: population 59,322

Lancaster was the original capital of Pennsylvania, until Harrisburg claimed that title in 1812. Central Market, located in Lancaster's Penn Square, is the nation's longest continuously operating farmer's market.

9. Harrisburg: population 49,528

Before European settlement, the capital city of Pennsylvania was an important crossroads for Native American traders. Harrisburg's economy was based on steel manufacturing, agriculture, and food services. Today, the U.S. government is one of its top employers.

10. Altoona: population 46,320

Altoona's founding and growth were closely tied to the Pennsylvania Railroad. Altoona is just a few miles from Horseshoe Curve, a manmade structure that allowed trains to travel more easily through the Allegheny Mountains.

Bethlehem

Pennsylvania chartered Penn State University in 1855. It was one of the country's first colleges set up to apply scientific principles to farming. It was built on 200 acres (81 hectares) donated by James Irvin of Bellefonte.

Founding president Evan Pugh and others urged congress to pass the Morrill Land-Grant Act in 1862. This act allowed states to sell land given to them by the federal government and to use the money they received to pay for colleges. Penn State is the **Commonwealth's** only land-grant university.

In colonial times, many Pennsylvanians owned slaves. Slavery gradually disappeared in Pennsylvania after a law against it was adopted in 1780. The state became one of the many safe places for freed or escaped slaves to start new lives. The Underground Railroad was a network of people who helped African-American slaves from the South escape to freedom in the North and in Canada, where slavery was illegal. Some historians estimate that more than 100,000 people tried to leave the South through the Underground Railroad. Many escaping slaves died along the way. Others were caught and taken back to their masters.

Locomotives such as the one above transported people and coal in Pennsylvania in the early 1800s.

However, many managed to make their way to freedom. The borough (a community similar to a town) of Columbia, along the Susquehanna River in Lancaster County, became a popular place for runaway slaves to settle.

A piece of the Underground Railroad was recently discovered in Columbia. Stone bridge piers and part of a lock on the Pennsylvania Canal were partially uncovered recently. The National Underground Network to Freedom run by the National Park Service stated these things were used to move slaves to freedom. These remains, which were part of the mile-long Columbia-Wrightsville Bridge and the lock built in the nineteenth century, are being restored. There are now eight sites in Columbia tied to the Underground Railroad, the most in the state.

One of the giants of the Underground Railroad was Daniel Hughes, and he was a very large man. He was at least six feet, seven inches tall (2 meters) and weighed about 300 pounds (136 kilograms). He moved north of Williamsport in 1828 to an area that has been renamed Freedom Road, and worked moving lumber on a river raft. He operated on the Susquehanna River between Williamsport and an area just north of Baltimore, Maryland. This job gave him the ability to smuggle slaves from

The Underground Railroad moved slaves through Pennsylvania to freedom up north. This sign is in Loyalsock Township.

FREEDOM ROAD CEMETERY

Daniel Hughes, a lumber raftsman on the Susquehanna, lived here, 1854-80. In the years ending with the Civil War, he brought fugitive slaves here from Maryland, protecting them before they continued north via the Underground Railroad. Hughes gave part of his land for a cemetery, and among those buried here are nine known African-American veterans of the Civil War. The cemetery has borne its present name since 1936.

PENNSYLVANIA HISTORICAL AND MUSEUM COMMISSION   1993

Boone for Hunting

Daniel Boone was a native of Pennsylvania but he is most remembered for his days as a woodsman in Kentucky. He was so skilled with his Pennsylvania Long Rifle while on extended hunts that the name of the gun was changed to the Kentucky Long Rifle.

Maryland, which allowed slavery, and central Pennsylvania.

Hughes would bring fugitive slaves up the river and hide them in a house in a wooded area or in caves on or near his property. His wife and sixteen children would sneak food to the fugitives before taking them to Trout Run for the next stop on the railroad in Elmira, New York.

They were often helped by the wealthy of Williamsport or people from local churches, mostly Quakers. Not one fugitive helped by Hughes was ever caught and returned to his owner.

The slavery issue was one of the reasons why the Civil War began in 1861. A total of eleven Southern states seceded—or separated—from the United States. They formed the Confederate States of America. Pennsylvania remained a part of the United States, which was also called the Union. The state sent more than 400,000 men to fight the Confederate forces. State residents provided supplies and food for the Union troops. Pennsylvania also produced much of the military equipment that was used.

Confederate and Union forces fought many bloody battles. One of the most famous was fought in Gettysburg, Pennsylvania, in 1863. The Battle of Gettysburg lasted from July 1 through July 3. About fifty thousand soldiers were wounded or killed, making the battle one of the bloodiest in U.S. history. Gettysburg marked the northernmost point that any Confederate army reached. Defeated there, the Confederates were forced to retreat. President Abraham Lincoln delivered his famous Gettysburg Address on the battlefield in 1863. This short but eloquent speech honored those who had fought and died for the country and its freedoms.

The South eventually surrendered to the North in 1865, and the war ended. The Confederate states rejoined the United States, the Thirteenth Amendment to the U.S. Constitution ended slavery nationwide, and the country started rebuilding and reuniting.

Through the end of the 1800s, Pennsylvania's economy continued to thrive. In addition to mining, manufacturing, and farming; there was oil—the discovery of oil in the northwestern corner of the state marked the beginning of the American oil industry.

Jobs were plentiful, and people from the war-torn Southern states, as well as immigrants from Scotland, Ireland, Russia, and Eastern Europe, came to Pennsylvania in hopes of making better lives. Work in the factories and mines, however, proved dangerous and did not provide as much money as the workers had expected. In the late 1800s, many of these workers demanded better pay and safer working conditions. Some of the first American labor unions were formed in Pennsylvania. These were groups of workers who banded together to demand better conditions and better pay.

The 1900s and Today

Pennsylvania continued to be one of the leading industrial states in the twentieth century. Unfortunately, in 1929 the Great Depression started, a severe downturn in the nation's economy that caused massive unemployment and hardship. Like many other states, Pennsylvania was hit hard. At one point, almost 80 percent of the workers at the state's steel mills and in its coal mines had lost their jobs. Since these were two of the biggest industries in Pennsylvania, the job losses meant that many people living in the state were unemployed. Without jobs, these workers had no money to feed their families or keep their homes. Most people could not afford to buy many products, so the merchants and farmers who provided these products to the public also suffered. Many people left the state to search for work elsewhere.

President Abraham Lincoln delivered the short but stirring Gettysburg Address on November 19, 1863.

Out of work miners marched in Washington, Pennsylvania, in 1931, seeking government aid.

The state and national governments set up programs to help. Workers were employed by government to build and fix bridges, highways, and dams. Others were paid to work in the forests.

In 1939, World War II began in Europe. The United States joined the war in 1941. As in World War I, in which the United States fought from 1917 to 1918, the state sent many soldiers to serve in the military. Pennsylvania mines and factories also provided supplies for the war effort. Workers were hired to operate the steel mills, factories, and coal mines.

After the war, the state's economy prospered for a time, but then demand for Pennsylvania steel and coal declined, and many factories were shut down. It took many years, but the state's economy eventually bounced back.

One improvement occurred in 1973. The Harley-Davidson motorcycle assembly operation, which had built nearly ninety thousand motorcycles for the United States military during World War II, was moved to York, Pennsylvania. The company opened a museum in York which includes a Kids Corner. The museum allows visitors to learn how these vehicles are made.

While mining and manufacturing continued to some extent, other areas of the economy, such as services, became more significant. New industries became important, including the computer industry. Pennsylvania played an important early role in their development. ENIAC, the first large-scale general-purpose electronic digital computer, was built in Philadelphia at the University of Pennsylvania in 1946. The Remington Rand Corporation, also in Philadelphia, made the first commercial computer, the Univac I, in 1951.

That first computer was delivered to the U.S. Census Bureau. In 1952, it was used by CBS News to accurately predict the outcome of the presidential election. The company became Sperry-Rand in 1955 and ultimately was renamed Unisys. Located in Blue Bell, the company employs more than twenty-two thousand people and sells billions of dollars' worth of technology goods and services.

In part as a result of the state's reliance for many years on mining and manufacturing, Pennsylvania's environment suffered, and air and water pollution were serious problems. This was especially true in Pittsburgh, where a lot of steel was made. However, in recent decades, the state's air and water have generally become cleaner. Partly this was a result of changes in the state's economy. A very important factor was also the passage of state and federal laws protecting the environment.

The Univac I, the first commercial computer, was made in Pennsylvania in 1951.

However, a petition filed by Ashley Funk of Mount Pleasant to regulate carbon dioxide emissions in the state was rejected in August 2014 by the Pennsylvania Environmental Quality Board. Ashley, who was eighteen when she filed the petition, says she is trying to take action against climate change. The state has a Climate Change Action Plan but it reportedly does not tell companies how much they should cut carbon dioxide emissions. Ashley's petition asked for a 6 percent reduction each year until 2050.

President Barack Obama announced his own plans to combat climate change in 2013. They would require Pennsylvania—which emitted the third-highest carbon dioxide rate in the country—to reduce emissions by 30 percent by 2030. The president also promoted the use of renewable energy, and Pennsylvania was among thirty-five states to have set targets for renewable energy use.

The state has also taken action to preserve the many historic sites and landmarks that are part of the heritage of Pennsylvania.

10 KEY DATES IN STATE HISTORY

1. 1682
William Penn establishes the colony of Pennsylvania.

2. July 4, 1776
The Declaration of Independence is adopted in Philadelphia at Independence Hall. The document was signed about a month later.

3. December 12, 1787
Pennsylvania becomes the second state to ratify the new U.S. Constitution, which was written at the Constitutional Convention in Philadelphia.

4. July 1-3, 1863
Union forces defeat the Confederates in the Battle of Gettysburg during the Civil War, ending the last Southern and the deepest advance onto Northern soil during the war.

5. May 31, 1889
A massive flood, caused by failure of the South Fork dam on the Little Conemaugh River, kills more than 2,200 people in the Johnstown area. It was the first disaster aided by the new American Red Cross.

6. October 2, 1940
The first section of the Pennsylvania Turnpike opens. It includes two-lane tunnels at Laurel Hill, Allegheny, Ray's Hill, Sideling Hill, Tuscarora, Kittatinny, and Blue Mountain.

7. December 2, 1957
The first U.S. full-scale nuclear power plant goes into service in Shippingport.

8. March 28, 1979
An accident at the Three Mile Island nuclear power plant causes widespread concern.

9. September 11, 2001
United Airlines Flight 93, hijacked by terrorists, crashes in a field near Somerset. The Flight 93 National Memorial has been built on the site to honor passengers who prevented the terrorists from flying the plane into the U.S. Capitol.

10. January 22, 2012
Joe Paterno, head coach of the Nittany Lions football team at Pennsylvania State University from 1966 to 2011, dies of complications from cancer.

A dancer wears traditional dress at a powwow in Sullivan County.

The People

3

M uch like the variety found in its climate and landscape, Pennsylvania also has a diverse group of residents from many cultures. In 1790, when the first **census**, or count, of all the people in the United States was taken, the population of Pennsylvania was almost 435,000. Sixty years later, the number of people living in Pennsylvania had dramatically increased to more than two million. The number of residents continued to grow rapidly. In 2010, the U.S. Census Bureau estimated that Pennsylvania had a population of more than 12.7 million people. The bureau also reported that the people of Pennsylvania come from a wide variety of cultures.

The First Residents

Native Americans hunted, farmed, and lived for centuries on the land that is now Pennsylvania. Major groups in the region when the first Europeans arrived included the Iroquois, Susquehannock, Shawnee, and Lenape. Loss of land and hunting grounds, European settlement, and diseases brought by the Europeans decreased the population of indigenous people in the region.

The U.S. Census Bureau estimated that in 2010, Native Americans accounted for only about 0.2 percent of the state's population. Today, there are no federally recognized Native American reservations in Pennsylvania. However, many Native Americans from different

Who Pennsylvanians Are

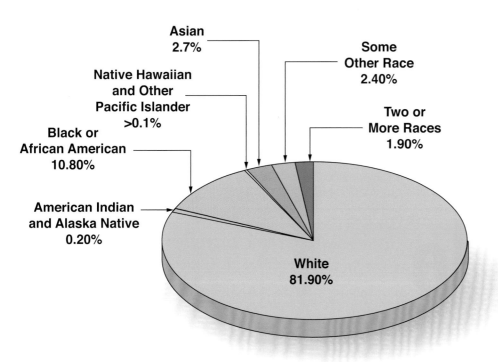

Asian
2.7%

Native Hawaiian
and Other
Pacific Islander
>0.1%

Black or
African American
10.80%

American Indian
and Alaska Native
0.20%

Some
Other Race
2.40%

Two or
More Races
1.90%

White
81.90%

**Total Population
12,702,379**

Hispanic or Latino (of any race):

• **719,660 people (5.7%)**
Note: The pie chart shows the racial breakdown of the state's population based on the categories used by the U.S. Bureau of the Census. The Census Bureau reports information for Hispanics or Latinos separately, since they may be of any race. Percentages in the pie chart may not add to 100 because of rounding.

Source: U.S. Bureau of the Census, 2010 Census

tribes and nations live in the state. Native Americans in Pennsylvania own farms, have jobs in towns and cities, and hold office in local and state governments. Throughout the year, festivals and powwows (Native American fairs, with dancing and more) take place across the state. Pennsylvania also has many historical landmarks and museums dedicated to indigenous people.

The Pennsylvania Dutch

The people known as the Pennsylvania Dutch are descendants of European immigrants who spoke a form of German ("Deutsch"). They are not descendants of Dutch people from Holland. Their ancestors began coming to Pennsylvania in the seventeenth century. Many wanted to get away from wars in Europe and find religious freedom in a new land. By 1775, the Pennsylvania Dutch made up one-third of the colony's population. Today, a large proportion of the Pennsylvania Dutch live in the Lancaster area, where they are estimated to number close to 100,000 people. Many of them belong to such Christian branches as the Amish, Mennonites, and Brethren.

Some Pennsylvania Dutch live in much the same way as their ancestors. They do not believe in modern conveniences such as electricity or cars. They run their farms in nearly the same manner as their ancestors did centuries ago. On some roads in Lancaster County,

Pennsylvania Dutch horse-drawn carriages can be seen alongside cars. However, not all Pennsylvania Dutch live in seventeenth- or eighteenth-century conditions. Some people of Pennsylvania Dutch descent use all types of modern technology and conveniences.

Lancaster County in southeastern Pennsylvania is home to the second-largest population of Amish people in the world. (Only the Holmes County area in Ohio has more Amish.) In Lancaster County and in some other parts of the state, people can visit museums and historic farmhouses that share the history and culture of the Pennsylvania Dutch.

Keeping in Contact

Owning a telephone is against strict Amish beliefs, but using one is not. Many Amish will use a "community phone" shared by several neighboring families to contact doctors, dentists, or veterinarians, and make other important calls.

A Mix of Cultures

According to the U.S. Census Bureau, as of 2010, Pennsylvania's population was about 82 percent Caucasian, or white. Some are descended from the earliest European settlers:

This Iroquois family was photographed around 1900.

10 KEY PEOPLE ★ ★

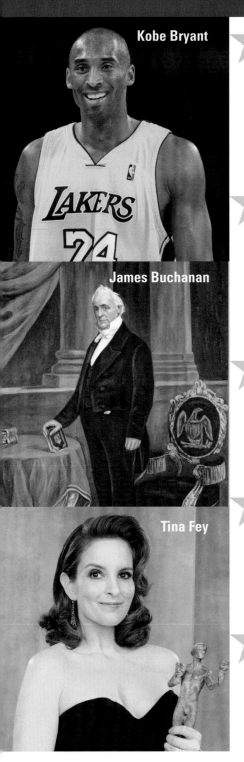

Kobe Bryant

James Buchanan

Tina Fey

1. Kobe Bryant

Kobe Bryant went directly from Lower Merion High School to the National Basketball Association in 1996, becoming the twenty-seventh player to do so. At the end of the 2014 season, he was among six players to have topped thirty thousand career points.

2. James Buchanan

The fifteenth president of the United States, from 1857 to 1861, was born in 1791 in Franklin County. Before becoming president, Buchanan was a U.S. congressman and senator, ambassador to Great Britain, and the secretary of state under President James K. Polk.

3. Rachel Carson

Born in 1907 on a farm near Springdale, Rachel Carson's main concerns were studying, preserving, and protecting the environment. Her book, *Silent Spring*, pointed out the health dangers of pesticides.

4. Bill Cosby

As a comedian and actor who is African American, the Philadelphia-born Bill Cosby has been able to overcome prejudice and bring attention to the similarities—rather than the differences—among people of different backgrounds.

5. Tina Fey

The career of Tiny Fey, raised in Upper Darby, has included writing and co-starring in television shows and films such as *30 Rock*. In 2010, at the age of forty, she became the youngest person to receive the Mark Twain Prize for American Humor.

PENNSYLVANIA

6. Gene Kelly

The son of Irish immigrants who settled in Pittsburgh, Gene Kelly sang and danced his way to stardom. His most famous movies are *An American in Paris* and *Singing in the Rain*.

7. Tara Lipinski

Born in Philadelphia in 1982, Tara Lipinski started ice skating when she was six. The youngest person to win the ISU World Figure-Skating Championship, she also became the youngest person to win an Olympic gold medal in figure skating in 1998.

8. Robert Peary

This explorer from Cresson is credited with being the first man to reach the North Pole on April 6, 1909. A rear admiral in the U.S. Navy, he was the first to find evidence that Greenland was an island.

9. P!nk

Born Alecia Beth Moore in Abington in 1979, P!nk began performing in Philadelphia clubs when she was fourteen years old. With nineteen albums reaching *Billboard's* Top Twenty, she has won three Grammy awards and six MTV Video Music awards.

10. John Updike

Author John Updike is the first American to win two Pulitzer Prizes for fiction. Born in Reading and raised on a farm near Plowville, he earned a National Book Award for his novel *The Centaur*, which is about his childhood in Pennsylvania.

Gene Kelly

Tara Lipinski

P!nk

the Dutch, the Swedish, and the English. Other Caucasian residents can trace their ancestors to the German, Polish, Italian, Irish, Scottish, and other immigrants who came to the state over the centuries. New European immigrants, as well as Americans with European backgrounds who relocate from other states, continue to move into Pennsylvania and make it their home.

Today, African Americans make up the largest minority group in the state. Approximately a tenth of the population is African American. Between 1780 and 1847, slavery was gradually ended in Pennsylvania. Many freed slaves chose to live in and around Philadelphia and other Pennsylvania cities. Many of their descendants make Pennsylvania their home today. In the twentieth century, many African Americans from the South settled in the state. This was especially true in the years after World Wars I and II. Many factory and other industrial jobs were available in Pennsylvania at that time, and workers in these jobs tended to earn more money than, say, people who worked on farms in the South.

The Amish travel and live in traditional ways in Pennsylvania.

Hispanic and Asian Pennsylvanians

More than 700,000 Hispanic people live in Pennsylvania. Hispanics started moving to the state in the nineteenth century. Some came as experienced farmers and found work in agriculture. Others found jobs in different lines of work, and many opened their own businesses. Many came from Puerto Rico. In recent years, the Hispanic population has grown rapidly to include people from Mexico, Cuba, the Dominican Republic, and other countries. In many of Pennsylvania's cities, you can find businesses, restaurants, and stores owned by Hispanic Americans. Throughout the year in different parts of Pennsylvania, residents hold festivals and other events celebrating Hispanic culture.

Asian Americans make up almost 3 percent of the state's population. The state's Asian population includes people of Indian, Chinese, Filipino, Vietnamese, Korean, and Japanese heritage. Some of these people are the children or grandchildren of immigrants who came to the state many years ago. Others are new residents. Regardless of how long they have lived in the state, their influence can be seen in different parts of Pennsylvania.

Students learn about their cultural traditions in Pennsylvania schools.

Italian Immigration

Between 1880 and World War I, thousands of Italian people immigrated to the United States to find work in Pennsylvania, with the majority moving to Pittsburgh or Philadelphia. In 1870, there were only 784 Italian-born people living in Pennsylvania. By 1910, that number had increased to more than 190,000.

Philadelphia has a thriving Chinatown. This part of the city first attracted Chinese immigrants who arrived more than one hundred years ago. Through the years, visitors and residents have enjoyed—and continue to enjoy—Chinatown's shops, restaurants, and cultural celebrations.

Celebrating Traditions

Historically, Pennsylvania has always been known as a place where people from many different backgrounds and cultures gathered. Through the years, the racial and ethnic makeup of Pennsylvania's people has changed. This diversity has helped make Pennsylvania into the appealing state that it is today.

The Mummers Parade on New Year's Day is a Philadelphia tradition.

Some of Pennsylvania's best-known traditions have their roots in the state's immigrant heritage. Philadelphia's highly popular Mummers Parade is one example. Held every year on January 1, the parade features bands and other marchers in fancy and colorful costumes. The origins of this event go back to the customs of the region's early Swedish settlers, who would celebrate the New Year by dressing up in elaborate costumes and walking through the streets ringing bells and visiting friends. By the beginning of the twentieth century, this practice had evolved into an organized parade. Today, more than forty social clubs in the Philadelphia area provide the parade's thousands of marchers, and tens of thousands of people line the parade route to enjoy the show.

Pennsylvanians of various ethnic backgrounds enjoy celebrating their heritage. Irish Americans and others turn out for the annual St. Patrick's Day parades in Philadelphia, Pittsburgh, and other cities around the state. Philadelphia's Columbus Day parade honors the heritage of the area's Italian Americans. An annual Polish-American festival is held at the National Shrine of Our Lady of Czestochowa in Doylestown.

Reduced Representation

Pennsylvania's population rose 3.4 percent from 2000 to 2010. However, the U.S. population rose 9.7 percent during that same time period, leading Pennsylvania to lose one seat in the U.S. House of Representatives.

There is an annual Polish-American festival held at the National Shrine of Our Lady of Czestochowa in Doylestown.

10 KEY EVENTS ★

Applefest

Groundhog Day

Little League World Series

1. Applefest

This three-day event in Franklin is the largest crafts festival in western Pennsylvania. Starting the first Friday in October, the festival attracts over 300,000 attendees to enjoy apple eating contests, a classic car show, 5K run, and other entertainment.

2. Groundhog Day

On February 2, people flock to Punxsutawney to learn if Punxsutawney Phil, the event's official groundhog, will come out of his hole and see his shadow. If he does, you can expect six more weeks of winter.

3. International Chainsaw Carvers Rendezvous

An average twenty-five thousand people head to Ridgway every year to view some of the world's most talented artists who use chainsaws to create sculptures out of wood. The festival includes carving competitions, safety classes, an auction of chainsaw art, and more.

4. Little League World Series

Williamsport is the birthplace of Little League Baseball, which began in 1939. Every August, the Little League World Series is held in neighboring South Williamsport, which also has a Little League museum.

5. Mummers Parade

On the first day of January, Philadelphia holds its internationally famous Mummers Parade, featuring clowns, fancy costumes, dancing, and music. String bands provide the music, and the crowd is invited to do the Mummers Strut, a comical squat-kneed dance.

PENNSYLVANIA

6. Native American Autumnal Festival

Every September, this festival is held at the Indian Steps Museum in Airville, west of Philadelphia. The museum has one of Pennsylvania's largest collections of Native American artifacts, including arrowheads and tomahawks. One of the highlights is a powwow.

7. Odunde Festival

Attracting up to 500,000 people each June, the Odunde Festival is the longest-running and largest African American street festival on the East Coast. Spread over twelve city blocks in Philadelphia, the festival features two stages of live entertainment and more.

8. Pennsylvania Farm Show

More than ten thousand farm animals are on display at this Harrisburg event, the largest indoor agricultural fair in America. Over 400,000 attendees attend each January to see competing exhibits, educational displays and livestock shows.

9. Philadelphia Flower and Garden Show

The largest and oldest indoor flower show in the world, the Philadelphia Flower and Garden Show features plants grown around the world, as well as hundreds of vendors selling plants, flowers, floral-inspired artwork, crafts, and supplies.

10. Thunder in the Valley®: Annual Motorcycle Rally

Johnstown is home to this event that brings more than 100,000 motorcycle enthusiasts to the region during the fourth week of June. Attendees can hear live musical acts, and purchase accessories, helmets, clothing, and more.

Odunde Festival

Pennsylvania Farm Show

Philadelphia Flower and Garden Show

The legislature
meets in the
State Capitol in
Harrisburg.

4

How the Government Works

Pennsylvania is one of four U.S. states that are officially called commonwealths. (The other three commonwealths are Kentucky, Massachusetts, and Virginia.) The word commonwealth reflects the state's concern for the wellbeing of all its citizens. The word can mean a group of people (for example, all Pennsylvanians) who join together to promote their common good.

Pennsylvania is represented in the U.S. Congress in Washington, D.C. Like all states, Pennsylvania has two members in the U.S. Senate. The number of members each state has in the U.S. House of Representatives is related to the state's population and can change after each U.S. census is taken. As of 2014, Pennsylvania had eighteen representatives in the U.S. House.

Local Government

The state is divided into sixty-seven counties. A county is made up of several cities or smaller communities, which are called boroughs or townships. Each county has its own government, usually run by commissioners. These commissioners handle issues that affect the many communities within the county. However, each city, borough, or township also has its own local government. Local officials are elected by the residents of the community. Most cities and boroughs are run by a mayor and a council, or group of officials. Townships are managed by commissioners or by supervisors. City, borough, and township governments are designed to address local problems. Such issues as local budgets and land use are managed by these units of governments. The public school system is managed by separate units of government called school districts.

Many Pennsylvania residents are active in local government. Some serve as officials. Many attend numerous meetings and hearings that address local problems. Through elections, in which they choose public officials and decide important issues, local residents are able to control how their community is run.

State Government

The state government is responsible for issues that affect the state as a whole. The job of state officials includes drafting, approving, and enforcing laws; managing state budgets; and handling issues between Pennsylvania and other states and between Pennsylvania and the

A statue of Benjamin Franklin sits atop Philadelphia's City Hall, which was completed in 1901.

federal government in Washington, D.C. The center of the state government is the capital, Harrisburg, the state capital since the early nineteenth century.

Pennsylvania's state government is divided into three branches, which have different roles to play in governing the state. The executive branch is headed by the governor: the state's chief executive, or chief manager. The legislative branch passes laws for the state. The judicial branch includes the state's courts, which apply the laws to specific cases and may also decide whether a state law agrees with or violates the state constitution.

The Pennsylvania constitution describes the structure of the state government and the powers of each branch of government. The state constitution also sets limits on the powers of government. This protects the rights of individuals. Pennsylvania has changed its constitution several times in the course of the state's history. The current constitution was adopted in 1968.

How a Bill Becomes a Law

The ideas behind new laws can come from different places—sometimes from legislators and sometimes from state residents. A state resident with an idea for a law can present it to his or her state representative or senator. A proposed law is called a bill. For example, one bill might increase taxes to help pay for road repairs. Another bill might require harsh

The dome caps the beautiful interior of the State Capitol.

Court Steps In

In 2012, a law known as Act 13 said that local governments in Pennsylvania would have to obey statewide laws related to oil and gas mining, rather than enforcing their own regulations. Many environmental groups said the law was unfair to local communities. In 2013, the Pennsylvania Supreme Court made some portions of the law inactive.

punishments for people who commit very serious crimes. Other bills define people's jobs, such as the role of volunteer firefighters.

The state senator or representative originating a bill first takes it to the Legislative Reference Bureau. The bureau writes it in official legal language, making the bill ready for formal presentation. The bill is then given a name and number. It is first presented in the house in which it originated. This means that if a state representative helped draft the bill, it is first presented in the state house of representatives.

If the bill came from a senator, then the presentation starts in the state senate. The bill is introduced and then sent to a committee within the house or senate. The committee carefully studies the bill. Its job is to decide whether the bill should go to the whole house or senate to be voted on. The committee members base their decisions partly on public opinion. They may hold hearings to see how the public feels about the bill. If the committee finds that the public likes some of the ideas contained in the bill but not other parts of it, then changes—or **amendments**—can be made. Ultimately, the committee may decide not to send the bill to all the members of the general assembly. If a bill is rejected by the committee considering it, it is said that the bill has "died in committee."

However, if the committee concludes that the bill is worthy, it will send the bill to the entire house or senate for further consideration. At this time, representatives or senators debate the merits of the bill and have a chance to change the bill by suggesting amendments. They then vote on the bill. If the bill is passed by a majority vote, it moves on to the other half of the general assembly. There, the same process is carried out. If both houses can agree on the final bill and any amendments that were made, it is passed to the governor.

The governor reviews the bill and must decide whether to approve it or veto it. If he or she approves, it becomes law. A bill that is vetoed by the governor can still become a law. For that to happen, the bill must be passed again by a two-thirds majority of each house of the general assembly.

The state encourages its residents to take an active part in their government. Many hearings are open to the public. Pennsylvanians can voice their concerns and give suggestions to their state legislators. Many legislators invite their constituents—that is, the residents they represent—to visit them at the State Capitol to learn more about the state government and its processes.

The Pennsylvania House of Representatives meets in this chamber.

Branches of Government

EXECUTIVE

The governor is the head of the executive branch. He or she is elected to a four-year term and cannot serve more than two terms in a row. The governor's responsibilities include approving or vetoing (rejecting) proposed laws and supervising the state budget. The executive branch also includes officials who work with the governor, such as the lieutenant governor, attorney general, and state treasurer.

LEGISLATIVE

The legislative—or lawmaking—branch is the general assembly. Two houses make up the general assembly: the senate and the house of representatives. Senators serve four-year terms, and representatives serve for two years. There are fifty senators in the general assembly and 203 representatives.

JUDICIAL

The judicial branch is responsible for making sure that laws are followed. The state supreme court heads this branch. This court has seven justices, who are elected to ten-year terms. Lower courts include the appellate courts (the superior court and the commonwealth court), the courts of common pleas, and the community courts. These courts are often limited to certain types of cases, based on the kind of crime or other matter involved.

POLITICAL★FIGURES
FROM PENNSYLVANIA

Benjamin Franklin: Founding Father

Born in 1706, Ben Franklin was a printer, author, inventor, scientist, educator, and politician. He served in the Continental Congress, was a delegate to the Constitutional Convention in 1789, and signed the U.S. Constitution. Benjamin Franklin died in Philadelphia in 1790.

Tom Ridge: Director of Homeland Security, 2003–2005

Tom Ridge served in the United States House of Representatives, and as the forty-third governor of Pennsylvania. After the terrorist attacks on September 11, 2001, he became the first United States Homeland Security Advisor, and in 2003, the first Secretary of Homeland Security.

Arlen Specter: United States Senator, 1989–2010

A top staffer on the Warren Commission in 1964, Arlen Specter helped investigate the assassination of President John F. Kennedy. He served as Philadelphia District Attorney before winning the first of five consecutive terms in the Senate in 1979.

PENNSYLVANIA
YOU CAN MAKE A DIFFERENCE

Contacting Lawmakers

To get the contact information for the legislators representing a particular area in Pennsylvania, visit **www.legis.state.pa.us**

To find out what bills are being considered in the general assembly, visit **www.legis.state.pa.us/cfdocs/legis/home/session.cfm**

To find congressmen who represent Pennsylvanians in Washington, visit **www.govtrack.us/congress/members/PA**

You Can Make a Difference

When a politician is elected to office, they have a duty to represent the best interests of the state's residents. Your duty as a citizen is to participate in the lawmaking process by contacting your local lawmakers to express your support or concern for the bills and laws they are trying to pass.

In Pennsylvania, the strong reaction by citizens to a law passed in 2012 resulted in a law being struck down, or made inactive. The law required residents to show photo identification when they voted. Supporters of the law said it would prevent voter fraud. However, many Pennsylvanians protested the law, saying it was unfair and would prevent people who did not have identification from exercising their right to vote.

Citizens who did not support the law contacted their lawmakers with letters, emails, and phone calls, and some even held protests in the state capital. Partly because of the strong reaction from the public, the state supreme court struck down the law in early 2014.

If you have an opinion about the laws in Pennsylvania that you'd like to share with your state representatives, visit **www.legis.state.pa.us**. Under "Find My Legislator," click on "Your Address" and type in your address. If a law applies only to the area you live in, look up the website for your town or county to find contact information for those elected officials.

To contact national representatives, go to the website listed above and click on the representative's or senator's name. There will be contact information on that page.

The first Hersey's Kisses were produced in 1907.

HERSHEY'S
KISS
WORKS

Making a Living

Agriculture, mining, manufacturing, and service industries help keep Pennsylvania's economy running. They supply goods and services used around the world, and they provide jobs for millions of people in Pennsylvania.

Forests and Farms

Agriculture and other industries relying on natural resources have always played a large part in Pennsylvania's economy. The lumber industry was important during the eighteenth and nineteenth centuries. Millions of trees were harvested for lumber and for papermaking. As a result, Pennsylvania lost most of its forests. Today, much of the state is again covered by trees, and the forest-products industry again plays an important role.

Instead of the pine and hemlock trees that once covered the land, hardwoods such as black cherry, oak, maple, walnut, poplar, and ash now predominate. Pennsylvania is the country's leading hardwood producer, accounting for about a tenth of total U.S. output. Pennsylvania also has many Christmas tree farms, which grow pine trees for the holidays.

Unlike the lumber industry, Pennsylvania's farming industry has remained relatively steady through the centuries, although the area devoted to farming has tended to decrease in recent decades. Today, about one-fourth of Pennsylvania is farmland.

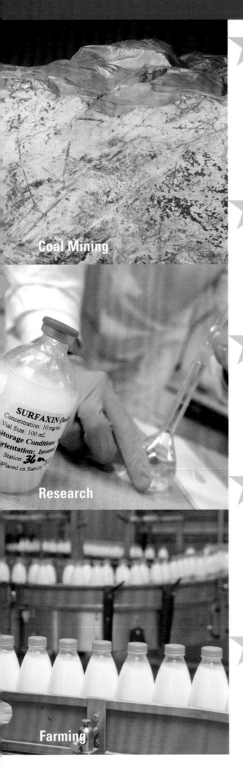

Coal Mining

Research

Farming

1. Chemicals

Chemical manufacturing is one of Pennsylvania's major industries. Especially important is the manufacture of drugs, or pharmaceuticals. The state accounts for more than a tenth of U.S. pharmaceutical output. Other chemicals produced include those used in paints and glues.

2. Coal Mining

Coal is one of Pennsylvania's most important and widely available resources. Pennsylvania was the fourth largest coal-producing state in the nation in 2012, mining 68 million tons that year, and it is the only U.S. state producing anthracite coal.

3. Education and Research

Many areas across Pennsylvania boast research institutions, universities and colleges as major employers and contributors to the local and state economy. Pennsylvania State University alone generates more than $17 billion in annual economic impact.

4. Farming

More than sixty-two thousand farm families call Pennsylvania home. Farming-related services such as food processing, marketing, transportation; and farm equipment combine to make **agribusiness** one of the state's leading industries, contributing nearly $68 billion to Pennsylvania's economy.

5. Life Sciences

Pennsylvania's strengths in health care, education, and manufacturing have allowed its life sciences sector to thrive and have a direct impact on health, agriculture, medicine, and many other areas. In 2011, the **life sciences** industry in Pennsylvania employed nearly eighty thousand people.

6. Lumber

Although 90 percent of Pennsylvania was forest when it was settled, the lumber industry in the late 1800s and early 1900s left the state largely deforested. Significant **reforestation** efforts during the twentieth century have made Pennsylvania lumber an in-demand resource once again.

7. Manufacturing

Manufacturers account for 10 percent of Pennsylvania's workforce. In addition to traditional manufacturing of goods such as metal and machinery, a kind of production known as **advanced manufacturing**, related to new materials and technology, is a rising contributor to the state economy.

8. Natural Gas Mining

Natural gas mining has proven to be an important part of Pennsylvania's economy. A large rock formation under the state known as **Marcellus shale** is a large source of natural gas. Natural gas provides heat to approximately 38 percent of Pennsylvania homes.

9. Steel

For more than a century, steel manufacturing was the core of Pennsylvania industry. While the industry has suffered worldwide since the 1970s, steel still contributed more than $9 billion to Pennsylvania's economy in 2010.

10. Technology

Pennsylvania's research sector is a growing source of economic power. A process called **technology transfer** helps scientists develop new high-tech products.

Lumber

Natural Gas Mining

Steel

Pennsylvania farmers harvest wheat, oats, mushrooms, soybeans, potatoes, and corn. Many acres are dedicated to apple orchards. Farmers in the southern part of the state grow tomatoes, grapes, peaches, and strawberries. Pennsylvania also produces cut flowers, shrubs, and ornamental trees for use across the country.

Animals raised in the state include hogs, sheep, and poultry. On many eastern and southeastern Pennsylvania fields, you might find herds of beef cattle grazing. Cows are also important to the dairy industry. Some Pennsylvania farmers raise llamas. Their hair can be used for clothing, and they can be trained to guard sheep herds.

Pennsylvania grasslands are great for cattle grazing.

Mining

Mined products include limestone, used for cement and other construction products. Many construction companies also use sand and gravel from the state. Pennsylvania coal is used for processing iron ore, heating homes, and generating electricity at power plants.

Coal is still one of Pennsylvania's most important products, but mining can cause problems for the environment. A fire broke out in 1962 in abandoned coal mines under Centralia, in the eastern part of the state. Efforts to put out the fire failed. The worst mine fire in the United States was still burning more than fifty years later, and almost all of the town's residents had left.

In 1859, the first U.S. oil well was dug in Titusville. Small amounts of oil continue to be produced in the western part of the state. Mining of natural gas with an environmentally controversial method known as **hydraulic fracturing**, or fracking, is a significant source of revenue for Pennsylvania as well.

Manufacturing

Andrew Carnegie came to the United States from Scotland with his family in the 1840s, when he was twelve, and the family settled in the Pittsburgh area. As a young man, Carnegie worked for the Pennsylvania Railroad, where he was promoted to increasingly important positions. He also invested money in other industrial companies.

In the 1870s and 1880s, he started or purchased several steel mills, which he combined into the Carnegie Steel Company. There was an increasing need for steel at that time for buildings and industrial equipment. Carnegie Steel became one of the largest steel manufacturers in the country, and Andrew Carnegie became one of the richest Americans of his time. The company did not always treat its workers well. In 1892, when workers at Carnegie's Homestead mill went on strike to protest a wage cut, the strike was broken up with the aid of armed guards, and several people were killed in a fight between guards and strikers.

After he sold Carnegie Steel (for almost $500 million) in 1901, Carnegie donated hundreds of millions of dollars, largely to help establish numerous libraries, research

Recipe for Soft Pretzels

Pretzels are a favorite snack of Pennsylvanians. Have an adult help you with this easy recipe.

What You Need

Two .25 ounce (7 grams) packages
active dry yeast

1 cup (237 milliliters) warm water

3 1/2 cups (828 mL) all-purpose flour

2 tablespoons (29.6 mL) white sugar

1 tablespoon (15 mL) shortening,
melted

1 teaspoon (5 mL) salt

1 egg yolk

1 tablespoon (15 mL) water

coarse salt

What to Do

1. Have an adult help you preheat the oven to 375°F (190°C).

2. Stir yeast into 1 cup (237 mL) warm water in a large bowl. Stir in flour, sugar, shortening, and salt until it becomes dough.

3. Knead (push and pull with your hands) the dough for five minutes on a surface dusted with flour.

4. Place dough into a greased bowl and let rise in a warm place for about one hour.

5. Push the dough down and divide it into 12 equal-size pieces.

6. Roll each piece into a rope 18 to 20 inches (46 to 51 cm) long.

7. Shape your dough ropes into a pretzel shape and place on a greased baking sheet. Let pretzels rest for five minutes.

8. Stir the egg yolk with 1 tablespoon (15 mL) water in a small bowl until it is completely mixed. Brush yolk mixture over each pretzel; sprinkle each with coarse salt.

9. Bake for about fifteen minutes until pretzels are golden brown.

centers, and colleges—including part of what is now Carnegie Mellon University in Pittsburgh.

Pennsylvania's factories manufacture goods such as chemicals (including medicines), food products, computer and electronic products, tools, and paper. The milk from the state's dairy farms is processed and made into a variety of foods. Pennsylvania food-processing plants make cookies, cakes, crackers, bread, and other treats. The state's snack food and candy industry accounts for more than $5 billion in sales a year.

No First Lady

James Buchanan was the only president of the United States [1857-1861] who never married. In 1819, he was engaged to Ann Coleman, but the wedding was called off. Coleman died that same year.

Independence Hall in Philadelphia is one of the nation's most historic places.

Vacationers flock to the Delaware Water Gap National Recreation Area.

Services

Service industries include banking, health care, education, retail stores, restaurants, hotels, and government. More than three-fourths of workers in Pennsylvania are employed in such industries.

Tourism

Tourism is an important part of the state's economy. Millions of visitors come to Pennsylvania every year. They spend money on hotels, restaurants, and souvenirs. The tourist industry employs hundreds of thousands of Pennsylvanians.

Historic Pennsylvania draws tourists of all ages. Many travel to Philadelphia to see its colonial sites. Some sites, such as the Liberty Bell and Independence Hall (where the Declaration of Independence was approved and the Constitution was written), are located downtown in Independence National Historical Park. Civil War enthusiasts visit Gettysburg. One of the worst disasters in U.S. history is the focus of the Johnstown Flood National Memorial at St. Michael and the Flood Museum in Johnstown. Pennsylvania's rich railroad history is highlighted at places such as Scranton's Steamtown National Historic Site, which has one of the biggest collections of historic locomotives and rail cars in the United States.

Pennsylvania is home to many other museums and historical centers. Some of the best known are located in Philadelphia. These include the Franklin Institute (devoted to science), the Insectarium (for insect lovers), and the Philadelphia Museum of Art. Pittsburgh also has several popular and well-respected museums, including the Carnegie Museum of Natural History, the Carnegie Museum of Art, and the Fort Pitt Museum.

Pennsylvania's famed snack food industry is concentrated in the southeastern part of the state. Lovers of chips and pretzels are drawn to the many factory tours in York and Lancaster counties. The world's largest chocolate factory is located in Hershey. The Hershey Company dates its origin to 1894, when Milton Hershey, its founder, opened a candy plant in Lancaster. Tourists come to Hershey to learn about and sample the company's sweet treats. Visitors also spend time at the Hershey theme park, garden, wildlife park, and spa.

Professional sports are popular—and big business—in the state. Many Major League Baseball fans in Pennsylvania root for the Philadelphia Phillies or the Pittsburgh Pirates. When football season arrives, fans cheer for the Pittsburgh Steelers or the Philadelphia Eagles of the National Football League. In the National Hockey League, the Philadelphia Flyers and Pittsburgh Penguins skate for Pennsylvania's two largest cities. In professional basketball, the state has the Philadelphia 76ers of the National Basketball Association.

People are also drawn to Pennsylvania's wilderness. With more than 2.1 million acres of state forests, the Allegheny National Forest, and more than one hundred state parks, Pennsylvania is a haven for people who want to enjoy nature. Many families spend vacations amid the woods of the Poconos. The Delaware Water Gap National Recreation Area spans a forty-mile (64 km) stretch of the Delaware River, along the border of Pennsylvania and New Jersey. Visitors can enjoy swimming, fishing, canoeing, kayaking, and rafting, as well as hiking in the hills alongside the river.

PENNSYLVANIA
STATE MAP

Lake Erie

Presque Isle State Park
Erie
Warren
Bradford
Pymatuning Reservoir
French River
Erie National Wildlife Refuge
Allegheny National Forest
East Branch Clarion River Reservoir
Tioga State Forest
Franklin
Allegheny River
St. Marys
Susquehannock State Forest
Williamsport
Wilkes-Barre
Scranton
Delaware River
Delaware State Forest
Shenango River Lake
Maurice K. Goddard State Park
Clarion River
Moshannon State Forest
Pine River
Tioga River
Pocono Mountains
Delaware Water Gap National Recreation Area
Sharon
New Castle
Mahoning River
W.
Sproul State Forest
Sunbury
Hazleton
Hickory Run State Park
Blue Mountains
Butler
Mahoning Creek Lake
Allegheny Mountains
State College
Appalachian Mountains
Allentown
Bethlehem
Pittsburgh
Altoona
Little Juniata River
Rothrock State Forest
Jacks Mountain
Tuscarora State Forest
Juniata River
Mohantango Mountain
Reading
Schuylkill River
Johnstown
Raystown Lake
Appalachian Mountains
Tuscarora Mountains
Kittatinny Mountain
Gifford Pinchot State Park
Harrisburg
Valley Forge National Historical Park
Philadelphia
Washington
Monongahela River
You
Ohio River
Uniontown
Forbes State Forest
Mount Davis
Buchanan State Forest
Buchanan's Birthplace State Park
Chambersburg
Gettysburg National Military Park
Gettysburg
South Mountains
York
Susq
Lancaster
Delaware River

Legend

Interstate Highway	State Capital	Highest Point in the State
U.S. Highway	City or Town	Mountains
Pennsylvania Turnpike	Wildlife Refuge	National Forest
	State Forest	Military Park
	State Park	Historic Park
	Recreation Area	

miles 0 20

N W E S

PENNSYLVANIA
MAP SKILLS

1. **What are the three rivers that run through Pittsburgh?**

2. **What city was the site of a turning point battle in the Civil War, and is now the site of a national military park?**

3. **Which Interstate Highway runs east to west through the middle of the state?**

4. **Which river in eastern Pennsylvania flows from the state's northern border to its southern border?**

5. **Which mountain is just north of the state capital?**

6. **The mountainous region in the east has two mountain ranges. What are they called?**

7. **President James Buchanan was born southwest of this city.**

8. **The Valley Forge National Historic Park is close to which historic city?**

9. **Which river runs through the Delaware Water Gap National Recreation Area?**

10. **Which island in Lake Erie is a state park?**

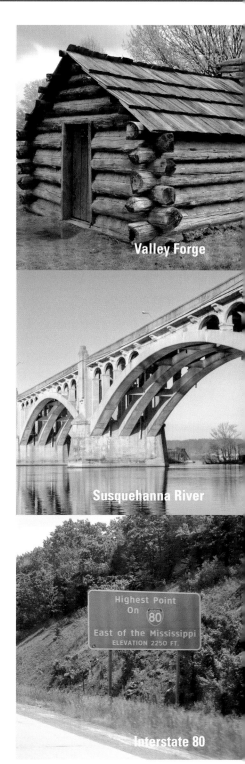

Valley Forge

Susquehanna River

Interstate 80

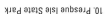

10. Presque Isle State Park
9. Delaware River
8. Philadelphia
7. Chambersburg
6. The Blue Mountains and the Pocono Mountains
5. Mohantango Mountain
4. Susquehanna River
3. Interstate 80
2. Gettysburg
1. The Allegheny, the Monongahela, and the Ohio

State Flag, Seal, and Song

Pennsylvania's state coat of arms is represented on the state flag. On each side of the coat of arms is a horse rearing up on its hind legs. An eagle sits above with its wings wide open. The state motto—"Virtue, Liberty, and Independence"—is beneath the coat of arms. In the center of the coat of arms are the same three symbols present on the state seal: a ship, a plow, and three sheaves of wheat. Below them are a crossed cornstalk and olive branch. Pennsylvania's state flag was officially adopted in 1799.

Pennsylvania's state seal was made official in 1791. The front shows a shield along with a sailing ship, a plow, and three sheaves of wheat. The ship stands for the commerce that developed by transporting goods by sea. The plow represents Pennsylvania's rich natural resources. The wheat symbolizes the state's fertile fields and the rich thought and action of its people. Above the shield is an eagle. Below the shield is a stalk of corn and an olive branch. The back side of the seal shows a woman holding a sword and trampling on a lion. It bears the motto, "Both Can't Survive." The woman represents liberty, and the lion stands for tyranny.

Pennsylvania's state song is called "Pennsylvania," and it was written and composed by Eddie Khoury and Ronnie Bonner. To learn the lyrics, visit: **www.50states.com/songs/penn**.

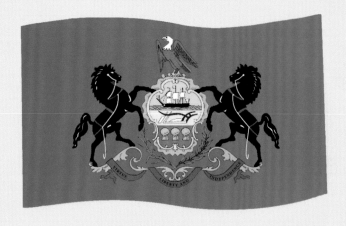

Glossary

advanced manufacturing	The use of innovative technology to improve products or processes. Advanced manufacturing plays an increasingly important role in Pennsylvania's economy.
agribusiness	The group of industries dealing with products and services related to farming. Agribusiness is one of Pennsylvania's largest sources of employment.
amendments	A change or addition to a legal document, such as a bill in the process of becoming law.
Amish	A group of people of German descent who avoid using most modern conveniences and technology. Pennsylvania's Lancaster County has a large population of Amish people.
anthracite coal	A hard coal that is plentiful in Pennsylvania.
census	An official count of the people who live in a specific area.
commonwealth	A community of people that join together to promote the common good. Pennsylvania is considered a commonwealth.
hydraulic fracturing	A mining technique that allows for drilling in rock formations. Hydraulic fracturing is used in Pennsylvania to harvest natural gas.
letterpress stamp	A tool to print images or letters by dipping a block with that image carved out into ink and pressing onto paper.
life sciences	Sciences concerned with the study of living organisms and have practical applications in medicine, technology; and many other fields. Life sciences are a growing part of Pennsylvania's economy.
Marcellus shale	The name of the rock formation that exists underneath much of Pennsylvania and contains rich resources of natural gas.
plateau	An area of relatively level high ground. Many plateaus can be found in Pennsylvania.
Quaker	A member of the Religious Society of Friends, a Christian movement founded circa 1650 and devoted to peaceful principles. William Penn, the founder of Pennsylvania, was a Quaker.
reforestation	The reestablishment of trees in an area where trees had recently been destroyed or removed.
technology transfer	The process of transferring skills, knowledge, technology, methods of manufacturing and more from research institutions to private industry or other organizations.

More About Pennsylvania

BOOKS

Armstrong, J. *A Three Minute Speech: Lincoln's Remarks at Gettysburg.* St. Louis, MO: Turtleback Books, 2003.

Figley, Marty Rhodes. *Who Was William Penn? And Other Questions About the Founding of Pennsylvania.* Minneapolis, MN: Lerner Publishing Group, 2012.

Jerome, Kate Boehm. *Pittsburgh and the State of Pennsylvania: Cool Stuff Every Kid Should Know.* Dover, NH: Arcadia Publishing, 2011.

WEBSITES

Pennsylvania's Official State Website
www.pa.gov

Pennsylvania's Official Website for Tourism
www.visitpa.com

Kid-Friendly Activities in Pennsylvania
www.4kidsinpa.com

ABOUT THE AUTHORS

Joyce Hart, whose grandparents came to Pennsylvania from Italy, has worked as an educator, an assistant librarian, an editor, and a desktop publisher. Currently she is a freelance writer and the author of several books. She has spent many years traveling the back roads of the United States.

Richard Hantula, based in New York, has worked as a writer and editor for more than three decades, during which he has crisscrossed Pennsylvania more times than he can remember.

Kerry Jones Waring is a writer and marketing specialist from Buffalo, NY. She took many trips through Pennsylvania when traveling between her hometown and Brooklyn, NY, where she earned a bachelor's degree in writing from Pratt Institute.

Index

Page numbers in **boldface** are illustrations.

Index